My Cash Value Life Insurance Is King!

Building Tax-Free Income Now, for a Financial Legacy Later

Dedication

This book is dedicated to all those who are on a mission to gain

information, knowledge, and financial literacy on their monetary

journey. It is written for first time wealth accumulators who are

interested in acquiring a blueprint for gaining control of their

money, having money for opportunities, and minimizing tax

consequences, while having the ability to build, acquire, and pass

wealth to future generations. This book is written for someone like

me, a first-time entrepreneur who knew nothing about money after

graduating college; and it is dedicated to all those on a journey

searching for the right information to be able to discover the things

about which they are most passionate.

When you understand what's going on, You will know what to do.

Jeff Moore

Acknowledgments

I want to give special acknowledgement to my wife Dezeree, my two daughters Samantha and Kierra, my parents Percy and Mary, who are now resting in the Lord, brother Kevin who is also resting in the Lord, and my family members all across the USA and Jamaica. Thank you, my friends for life: Calvin, Tony, Frank, Brian, Shelli, Chris, Kyle, Corey, Mike, Bruce, Courtney, Michelle, and my Penn State family who have been a constant source of love, motivation, inspiration, and support. My Pastors Ted and Dawn Winsley of The Family Church, NJ for their constant spiritual guidance and for helping me to have the attitude that winning is the best form of evangelism. My high school chess coach Edward McKinney, who provided me with support, guidance, encouragement, and the late Harold Rush who taught me that entrepreneurship was the key to generating real wealth. I also want to thank Bob Castiglione for teaching me how to put a moat around my financial castle, which gave me a greater appreciation of life insurance. My business partners Troy & Joyce Shorts for their support and more importantly introducing me to this wonderful opportunity and finally, I want to thank Mrs. Tangi Boone who inspired me to write this book after a telephone conversation on cash value life insurance.

Introduction

I see God bringing good out of this! My purpose in writing this book is to give you the information you need to pursue your passions and educate you on a few misperceptions out there regarding cash value life insurance. People want to be financially successful, but many do not know what they are supposed to do. The twin problems many entrepreneurs and professionals face are their lack of financial literacy and money management habits. This mismanagement of money has caused many to pay enormous fees, lose compound interest and pay more than their fair share of taxes, which puts additional pressure on how their money is saved and accumulated. I want to help communities of color build financial legacies because our dollars matter. I want to give you some insight and strategies to help you get control of your money, build massive savings accounts, earn uninterrupted compound interest, build tax free income at retirement, and leave a legacy for the next generation. It is also my desire to empower, educate and motivate you to adopt a financial system that will help you live the life you've imagined, as well as give you some information to expand your mindset and hopefully change your views on cash value life insurance. Many people in communities of color believe that life insurance cash value is the worst place to put your money, and that it's a terrible investment. They have the misperception that with life insurance you get nothing out of it because it only pays when you are dead. To say life insurance is for the dead is the most misrepresented statement heard often in our communities, and this book will give you a different perspective and change this narrative. You are not aware of the "living benefits' of life insurance. I'd like to change that.

Think of this book as your guide to build your foundation and to get you to understand the use and benefits cash value life insurance affords. This book is written to inspire you to act while giving you new information on how to incorporate the world's best product into your overall financial game plan. My intentions are to share some wonderful benefits cash value life insurance can have for you if you take immediate action! Cash value life insurance is the most powerful and important tool you can have to put a moat of protection around your money. Cash value life insurance is so valuable, the rich and wealthy uses it grow their wealth uninterrupted by market crashes, taxes, and even death. If cash value life insurance is good for the rich, then it has to be good for the middle class and the poor. Now is the time to "over-fund" (put every available dollar) into a cash value life insurance policy and watch it grow tax free while having access to the cash. Cash value life insurance is the most powerful asset you can own in your financial portfolio not because of what it is but what it does. This is the financial literacy and planning message that is missing in communities of color and this is the message I want to share to help close the wealth gap here in America.

I am going to shed some light on this darkness. I will break the problem down, then you will have a better perspective on how this strategy can work for you. You will feel more confident and prepared to get control of your money and make better financial decisions.

My goal over the next 10 years is to help 5,000 families create enormous cash value accounts to take advantage of opportunities in real estate, stocks, and businesses. This will help reduce risks and increase overall protection, while building an inheritance of billions of dollars for the next generations to enjoy and repeat. Please help me accomplish this goal by sharing this information with everyone you come across. I really encourage you to think about this amazing opportunity to have control over your money until your very last breath, provide certainty in an uncertain world and build tax-free income now, for a financial legacy later.

Contents

Section 1 – Mindset for Money

Rich people think like rich people and poor people think like poor people. The majority of people are bombarded by the media with mis information on how to save and accumulate money. The financial institutions spend billions of dollars in advertisements to get you to think one particular way. Their message is simple, give us your money, we will invest it for the long haul and you can have the profits of our strategies at retirement and we will transfer all the risk and all the fees over to you. Limited knowledge equals limited choices. The vast majority of people are confused about their money and where to put it. So many messages, so many theories, so many choices on where and how to position your money. Many are led astray believing the hype that the banks and financial institutions have their best interest at heart. I know, I was once caught up in the matrix. Here is my story.

The year was 2005, I was riding high. As a financial advisor I was working with clients and doing good. I was doing really good. As a matter of fact, I was coming off an economic financial high. I remember how proud I was. At 37 years old, I was debt free, a so called "hot-shot" "financial advisor with real estate investments, a mortgage broker business, and thriving shoes and clothing stores. I was doing and advising my clients everything the financial institutions taught me to do. Give them money; give them money on a continuous basis; let them hold on to this money for as long as possible and give back to you at the end very little as possible. Several of my friends referred to me as "Made-Man Jeff", because where I was born you only experienced this type of success if you were an athlete, entertainer, had a mean jump shot, or you sold crack cocaine. I was so proud of myself. I had recently gotten married, was starting my new family, and pursing the American Dream. One day as I was out house hunting and searching for our dream home, I stumbled across this beautiful house in New Jersey. The home was going on the real estate market in a matter of days but not listed on the real estate for sell listing. Since it had not yet been listed on the market, I moved quickly to purchase it. I can remember the look on my wife's face as she walked up the driveway. She wore this big ole' smile on her face while shouting "THIS IS IT!" before she even got a chance to see the inside. The asking price on the house was $599,000 and because I was able to negotiate a great price, we were able to move in with a sizable amount of home equity. We closed on the house quickly and the homeowners rented our place for three months until they secured their new home. The real estate market was hot. Home prices were booming. People were flipping homes and making money hand-over-fist. After entering into a partnership with a mortgage company, I was helping my clients purchase and refinance homes. I was working hard and having fun. Not only was my insurance and investment career rolling, I was helping my clients win by preaching over and over to save money, maximize your 401k and IRA plans, and have a diversified mutual fund. This is what I was taught to help people get on the path to achieving their financial dreams. Being a big believer in education, and investing in my personal development, I attended countless meetings and went to investment workshops. I read financial magazines and participated in mastermind groups. I knew that all that hard work and sacrifice would increase my knowledge, improve my skills, and make me more valuable in the industry. My motto is: *If I can get better, everything around me will get better.* The more value I can provide to the marketplace the more valuable I become, which leads to what? More money!

There was one conference in particular, which I attended in Florida, that changed everything. It's called The Lifetime Economic Acceleration Process (LEAP) conference that attracted many of the top financial advisors in the country. This conference had some of the most brilliant minds in the financial services industry. It was a four-day, strategy and knowledge fest with in dept workshops of how money really works. During this event, many of the elite producers taught strategies on how they maximize their client's overall protection and increased their wealth. The knowledge I learned from this conference disrupted all of the things the financial institutions taught. This was an eye-opening experience on how to get clients to learn how to save, accumulate, spend, and pass money to the next generation with tax advantages. I remember sitting in the conference center late one night discussing strategies on how to preserve wealth with an attendee from Utah. He was ecstatic that he was able to help his client recapture almost $250,000 in lost benefits through helping his client spend the death benefit on his life insurance policy while still living. This was the turning point in my financial services career. This conference inspired me to learn everything I could about money and life insurance. I left with several strategies on how to recapture cost and how the financial services and banks made money. It gave me the confidence I needed to help accelerate my career and serve my clients better. It was the apex that pivoted my mindset and changed my views on investing, accumulation, taxes and life insurance. I became fascinated about this new strategy and decided to learn everything I could on how to implement this strategy for myself, family and clients. I quickly adopted a plan of action for my wife and I, and as a result, 2005-2008 proved to be three of the best years of my working career then. I had no debt; I had plenty of money in the bank, real estate investments, and a diverse portfolio. I was riding high and feeling good. This is a big deal because, being a kid that grew up in North Philadelphia, this was not how my life was set to play out. Some of our elementary school teachers would tell me to "shut up, you don't know nothing and you aint going to be nothing". "Gaining knowledge is the first step to wisdom. Sharing it, is the first step to humanity". - Unknown

Mindset

"I AM" are the two biggest words in my mindset. Your mindset matters. As you think, you become. I am Loved. I am valued. I am appreciated. I have a big heart, I dream big. I am smart. I am passionate. I am secure. I am rich. I am special. I am an outside of the box thinker. I am creative. I am motivated by making money. I am motivated to help others. I am a teacher. But most importantly I am a Giver! These are some of the affirmations I repeat daily when I talk to myself.

Life is a measure of love, experiences, lessons, teachings, prayers, affirmations, exposure, and attitude. I am the youngest of eight children birthed from my mother, and second youngest child birthed from my father. I grew up in the inner city of Philadelphia where life comes at you very fast! I am from the hood, the real hood not the rap hood. I grew up poor, very poor. I am a momma's boy. My mother was passionate, compassionate, thankful, grateful, full of energy, and full of wisdom. I picked up all of these characteristics from her, and her constant love and support for me makes me the man I am today. I am very thankful my brother

Kevin taught me the game of chess at the early age of two, because the game of chess taught me how to strategically plan ahead, strategy and exposure. The game of chess was my escape out of the inner city. The game taught me strategy, positioning and more important how to win the end game. I am compassionate, I am smart, full of passion, full of energy, loyal, loud (very loud), and full of life. I am a giver. I have a big personality, I love to dream big, live large and I believe there are enough resources in the world for everyone to win. I believe everyone was born with special gifts and talents and I believe there is good in all people. Life is about strategy, relationships, mindset, exposure and how one can add value. I tell you a little about my background because I want you to gain some insight on how the lack of financial literacy, lack of financial education and leverage did not stop my will to win. Belief kills and Belief cures. My belief helps me to stay motivated and fuels my passion to get the message out that cash value life insurance is the best financial product on planet earth! You can't lose with the cash value I use. This is the only financial product that brings certainty in an uncertain world. My mother always told me that "When you understand what's going on, you will know what to do." My goal is simply to get you to understand the benefits of cash value life insurance so you will know what to do. Get as much as you can!!!

Let's face it. In order to have abundance and wealth, it starts in your mind. You are what you think about. It starts in your mind, travels through your heart, and is spoken out of your mouth. A successful money mindset is an overriding attitude that you will have success with your money in every area of your finances. This mentality will drive how you make key financial decisions every day and will have a big impact on your ability to save money, achieve your financial goals, and leave a legacy. The most important thing you can do is embrace a money mindset that will allow you to think of your money habits in a new and different way. I didn't have a money mindset early in life because I had no money. I discovered that if I wanted money, the way I viewed it would have to change. I started my money mindset by saying; I would save money before I spent money so I would always have money on hand. This mental adjustment of how I viewed money helped me to develop a positive mindset, and now my views about how I view my money has changed me forever. This has increased my confidence, and by following a few simple steps you can change your mindset and increase your money confidence as well.

- First, there will be no change until you change. You must totally believe your mindset can heavily influence your ability to save and manage money.

- Second, you must change your financial habits and start visualizing what's important to get control of the money that's coming under your management. What you believe about money determines all of the financial results you will have in your life.

- Finally, you must make a commitment to break the myths and negative views you have surrounding money and incorporate money affirmations to develop and build your money confidence. For example, are you saying things out of your mouth that can potentially ruin your money attitude and beliefs? Are you saying negative things or being influenced by negative money words that are stopping you from reaching your financial goals?

It is imperative that you develop a new money mindset that overrides this negative thinking you have about your money. Breaking these negative myths about money can have a big impact on your ability to achieve your money goals. If you change your mind set about money, you tend to make better choices about how to overcome the financial challenges you are having. The bible states that "A feast is made for laughter, wine makes life merry, and money is the answer for everything". This scripture is all about money thoughts and how you will use these money thoughts to build the Kingdom of God. Think better and you will have better! The subconscious mind is powerful because its primary function is to store and retrieve data. Its job is to ensure that you respond exactly the way you are programmed. Your subconscious mind makes everything you say fit a pattern consistent with your self-attitudes and beliefs. It doesn't know if what you are telling it is true or not, so say good things about your money and watch your money confidence soar! I am telling you this because I had to learn this lesson the hard way. As a kid growing up, so many negative things were said about money in my community. I always heard the old heads in the neighborhood say things like "I ain't got no money, don't ask me for nothing. I'm broke, I have to rob Peter to pay Paul. I can't find Peter, and Paul is knocking on my door saying, "Where is my money?" I am living paycheck to paycheck, so you must wait until I get paid. I have more bills than money." Most didn't have any money saved and would have to beg and borrow money when they came across a financial hardship. When the topic of life insurance came up, you would hear things like, "Why do I need life insurance? I won't be leaving anything to anyone because no one left me anything but debt." I'd also hear, "I am going to be dead … what benefit will I get from it?" The lack of positive money sayings, and the lack of money information, was appalling. I know many of you who are reading this can relate, but I am here to give you some information that can change your mindset and your views about your money and your life insurance!

Let's start with breaking some negative thinking about the lack of money. In order to change your views about your money, you must first change the views about how you see your money. **"There will be no change until you change."** That's the best piece of advice I could give to you.   One valuable way to Achieve this is by using "money affirmations". Challenge your mindset to do better! It just has to start in the mind so it can travel to the heart and be spoken out of the mouth! You cannot make more money or attract abundance into your life if you don't believe it. It starts with the mind. Your mind will change your attitudes and your views about money and the rest of the body will follow. These money affirmations changed my belief system and helped changed my inner dialogue I was having about my money. One word at a time. One sentence at a time. One story at a time. Rehearsed and repeated. We're all about creating a mindset that helps you go out and ACHIEVE. These money affirmations will do just that so repeat after me and go out there and ACHIEVE!

Affirmations:

- 1 am so happy and so grateful that money comes to me in increasing quantities from multiple sources on a continuous basis.

- I move from poverty thinking to abundance thinking.

- I save money before I spend money so I will always have money.

- My income is growing higher and higher.

- I attract money.

- I am rich.

- I am financially successful.

- I love money and money loves me.

- Money comes to me from unexpected sources and I am grateful.

- I receive money happily now.

- I am focused on becoming rich.

- My bank account is always growing. The more I enjoy life, the more money I make.

- I see abundance everywhere.

- I am a magnet for money.

- I happily see every bill paid.

- My income exceeds my expenses.

- Money is coming to me every day.

- I am aligned with the energy of abundance.

- I welcome an unlimited source of income and wealth in my life.

- Money is my servant.

- I have a positive money mindset.

- An avalanche of money is coming my way.

- Money creates a positive impact in my life.

- I am open and receptive to all the wealth life offers me.

- I am going to leave an inheritance for my kids, and my kid's kids.

- Money comes to me easily and effortlessly.

- Money expands my life's opportunities and experiences.

- I am the master of my wealth.

- I am at peace with having a lot of money.

- The more money I give, the more money I make.

- Financial Success is mine, I accept it now.

- I am able to handle large sums of money.

- I use money to better my life and the lives of others.

- I welcome an unlimited source of income and wealth in my life.

- Money expands my life's opportunities and experiences.

- My actions create constant prosperity.

- I am worthy of making more money.

- Money is the root of joy and comfort.

Do this as described and please remember my friend, all these affirmations will not produce any results if you don't put forth the effort to vividly visualize how you have already achieved the success that you desire.

Section 2: Money

My first introduction to money centered on the financial principles taught in the movie "Scarface". 1983 was the year. Get the money, then comes the power. Respect was all that was recited in the neighborhood I grew up in. Everything centered on making money. I don't recall any lessons on how to keep the money or to accumulate it. The talk was just about making it.

Later on, in life, the reasoning for the pursuit of money was to get it and flaunt it! Get the money, show off and let everyone know that you have it. Given my limited knowledge about money, this made perfect sense. As the years go on, the money game came from the financial institutions. Wells Fargo, Bank of America, Fidelity, JP Morgan Chase and Goldman Sachs are savages because they taught and trained that the best way to accumulate money is chase rate of return and to give up control. These losing strategies taught by the financial institutions through their agents, brokers and planners cost individuals billions of dollars of lost wealth, which they did not realize they were losing.

They tell you one thing and do another. One of the biggest lessons I observed was to keep the people confused. Where there is confusion, there is profit. Don't believe me, turn on your television set and you are bombarded with messages telling you to "buy this not stocks, not that one, maximize your 401k plan, why maximizing your 401k plan is a bad idea and a Roth 401k is better. 15-year mortgage is better than a 30-year mortgage. Prepay your mortgage and pay your home off faster, buy term insurance and invest the difference and my favorite don't buy whole life insurance because when you die the insurance company keeps the cash value". Lie, Lie, Lie! The lack of financial literacy has enabled millions of Americans to assume all the risk, give up control of their money and put the financial institutions in control to collect excessive fees. Can you say modern day robbery? I found this disturbing because a client could use this accumulating method, do all of the right things financially and still lose. The stock market could wipe it all out the day before you retire, or taxes can erode half of it. Question. Is there someone at the IRS that you are so madly in love with that you want to leave them a bunch of your money?

I am now on a quest to teach individuals how to get control over their money, recover wealth and create more wealth by creating more uses for their money. I have strategies that can help anyone position their money to win. This fuels my passion to learn more and bring more financial literacy to communities of color.

What should you do with your money?

Every day, you wake up and are faced with financial choices. The decisions you make with your money will have a direct impact on your life. Your decisions will dictate where you will go in the future, the person you will be, and the type of lifestyle you'll be living. One of the more difficult questions you will be faced with is, "What should I do with my money?" Every day you wake up, go to work, interact with family and friends, turn on the TV, read an article, or look at your phone, there seems to be an overwhelming number of options competing for your money. "Buy this, buy that, eat here, buy this course, put your money here, invest in this, buy this real estate, invest in this stock fund, do this investment right now and get rich," and on and on and on.... Before you can decide what, you should do with your money, you first need to know what you need your money to do for you. With money comes options, with options comes freedom, with freedom comes legacy! Let's discuss what your money should be doing for you and why having money is important to accumulate, spend, enjoy and pass along to your heirs. So, what should your money be doing for you? What can you do from now to increase your money IQ and develop a financial plan for success? What is the first thing you should do with your money?

You should save first: for emergencies, lifestyle and enjoyment. Second, give because givers get. Third, spend what you need to because that's why you save and accumulate it. And fourth, pass your fortune to your heirs.

- **Save First**, to protect your lifestyle. We live in a consumer-driven society. Saving your money is definitely better than spending it. Sometimes the hardest thing about saving money is just getting started. You have to start somewhere, and if you make a habit of it, your financial situation will improve. The first saving goal for most people should be a "what if" fund large enough to handle serious, unexpected expenses, such as your car breaking down, losing your job, or having a costly medical bill. I recommend having at minimum $3000 set aside with the goal of having at least six months of income. The more money you have saved, the more control you have over your financial life. Saving money first is worth the effort because it gives you peace of mind, options, and confidence because the more you do it, the better you get at it.

- **Save to Prepare for the Future.** Start saving early and let the magic of compound interest work in your favor. Future savings start with accumulating money. Saving money for your future is crucial. If you don't set savings goals and steadily work towards them, you will have to rely on others to take care of you in the future. Money is freedom when you have it. The more money you save, the more options you will have. The goal is to build and store as much money as you can to have guaranteed income for life. The goal is to live a lifestyle where you will never run out of money. No matter if you live to be 75 years old or live to be 120 years of age, you will not run out of money. The goal is to build and structure your money, so it reaches its highest level of accumulation without risk and fees. Save your money and your money will always save you. Build your fortune over a long period of time to create future income to spend on the things you are passionate about. This money is accumulated to enjoy the same lifestyle, or better, than your lifestyle when you were working and saving. Vacations, fine dining, concerts, travel, new experiences, enhancing relationships, doing the things you are passionate about, and making investments in you along the way is the primary goal for saving and accumulating money.

- **Save to Protect your Legacy.** Legacy is the amount of money or property left to someone in a will. Tis the season that we change the trajectory of our thinking to include what are we building for the next generation to enjoy and repeat throughout their lives.

Are we leaving a legacy of faith, business, property, and money; or are we leaving a legacy of debt and despair? We have to change the conversation and start giving future generations an opportunity to have a head start. This will position them to not have to worry about additional financial stresses that may hinder the development of their future dreams, goals and desires. It is my goal to end the days of financial setback for the next generation when replacement of income is lost at death. Write a will and decide who will get your assets and/or take care of your legacy when God calls you home. This will put you in the position to decide who benefits from all of your hard work.

Money myths that keep you from building wealth

Now that we are working to correct your thinking and get into the right mindset for financial success, it's time that we call out all of these long believed money truths for what they really are- myths that keep you transferring money away from yourself to other financial entities. Oftentimes, in our communities these long believed truths have stopped us from becoming the financial superstars we were intended to be. The financial institutions have done a particularly good job in getting us to believe these money truths and have conditioned us to rely on the banks and credit card companies. Let's dispel some money myths and get you back on the right track of being in control of your money and positioning your money to earn uninterrupted compound interest so you can build a pot of money to take advantage of opportunities that will build your wealth and give you the financial freedom you deserve. One of the biggest things I wished my parents would have taught me when I was a kid was to save money. This is one of the best habits everyone should learn at an early age. The younger the age, the better. Research from Cambridge University found that kids are already able to grasp money concepts between the ages of 3 and 4. By the age of 7, basic concepts relating to future financial behaviors will typically have developed. Money power and building wealth are developed by getting the right information and developing good savings habits early. We have been caught up in the misinformation hype and have been transferring our money away from us. Let's break this cycle and get the control of our money back into our hands. There is a lot of misinformation surrounding personal finance. I will debunk six money myths I hear when perspective clients have a consultation with me so you can focus on what matters. You don't need to have a big fancy job or a college degree from a top collegiate institution. When you eliminate these myths, money and success will eventually follow.

- **Money Myth #1: "I don't make enough to save."**
  This is the most common thing I hear talking with people regarding saving money and building wealth. Repeating and rehearsing this myth can be a scary situation and paralyze you from taking action. Gone are the days where you are overextending yourself with too much debt, no control over

your money, not having a budget, or not getting the financial literacy to build passive income. Today is the day we make a declaration to save money before we spend. When you save money before you spend money you will always have money. Who are you working for? You! So why aren't you paying yourself first? Next, commit to reducing your expenses. You can't put yourself in a position to save if you are spending everything you are making. These two simple adjustments will put you in a position where you will have the necessary money to save.

- **Money Myth #2: "Budgeting doesn't work for me, it's too difficult."** After you get into the habit of saving money, the next step is to break the myth that you don't need to work on establishing a budget. A budget is having a plan for your money. When you have a plan for your money, you can direct it where to go to handle your daily, monthly, or yearly financial obligations. You must be able to control the money that comes under your management. The idea of a budget not working for you, or your belief that budgeting is difficult, can kill your money aspirations. When I meet with potential clients and discuss their budget, many hate the idea of budgeting. It doesn't matter if they are making $40,000 per year or $400,000. The idea of tracking money is difficult, and many people fall into the myth that they can't live on a budget. In cases where the budget is not working, many of these potential clients are spending more money than they are bringing in every month, and it's frustrating. Some have experienced getting bank overdraft fees or had their credit card interest rates increased, all because they had the attitude that budgeting will not work for them, or thought budgeting was too difficult to abide by. In cases like this, I stress the need to change and create. Change the way you are viewing the money that's coming in under your management and create a budget. Creating a budget is not that difficult. For example, take out a pen and a piece of paper, write down all the money that's coming in and all the bills you have going out. If you need more help you can visit websites like mint.com, everydollar.com, or you needabudget.com. They all have free versions. Dive in and give budgeting a try. It's really not as difficult as you think it is.

- **Money Myth #3: Credit cards are good for emergencies.**
If I hear credit cards are good for emergencies again, I am going to scream! An emergency saving account with a debit card is good for emergencies, not credit cards. This is the biggest myth propagated by the credit card industry because they want your money. Every dollar you send to the credit card companies and pay an interest rate loses you the right to earn interest on that money forever. Using a credit card for emergencies is like getting a loan. If you can't afford to pay it back all at once, it means you'll have to pay interest. If you weren't already making monthly payments on this credit card, you'd be able to rid yourself of another monthly expense from your current budget. Besides, why would you want to put yourself at the mercy of the credit card issuer? Why not bank on yourself and create an emergency account to handle any unplanned emergencies. I suggest saving $3000 into an account as soon as possible. That's $60 per

week. $3000 should be enough money to handle if the car breaks down, pipes break or any other emergency at home.

- **Money Myth #4: "I can wait to start saving for retirement."** The reality is the longer you wait to start saving for retirement the more money you will need to save. The key years for saving have passed you by if you start saving in your 40's. Your best income producing years may still lie ahead but at age 40 you have many more demands on your money compared to your 20's. Kids, school tuition, family vacations, mortgage and car loans put serious demands on your money. Starting to save for retirement with your first job in your early twenties will give you 40+ working years to accumulate retirement dollars and let the magic of compound interest work in your favor! Let's put it another way. Let's assume you started investing in your early twenties, earned 8% in an account and wanted to save $1 million in your retirement account by the time you retired at age 67. You will need to save $166 a month for your retirement account, about $2,000 a year. If you waited until age 40 to start saving and wanted the same $1 million, you will need to save $880 a month. That's five times more than what you would have needed to save if you started in your 20's!

- **Money Myth #5: Borrowing money from your retirement plans is a good idea because you're borrowing money from yourself.** Borrowing money from your 401(k) is not necessarily damaging to your retirement savings because when you pay the loan back the payments goes back into your investment account. The interest you pay on the money borrowed goes back into the account so you're paying back more money into your account. On the surface it seems like a good idea, but what's rarely discussed is the double taxation you pay on your money. When you take pretax dollars (401(k) or 403(b) out in the form of a loan, the repayment must come from after-tax dollars (you paid taxes on this money to pay the loan back) and the 401(k)/403(b) monies will be taxed again at age 59 1/2 or retirement age when you take the money. Why would you knowingly pay taxes on the same dollar twice?

- **Money Myth #6 People believe math is money and money is math and it's not.**

Math is amazing and if you can understand math, you can win at almost anything! To understand math, we must first understand its meaning. The dictionary definition states that math is the systematic treatment of magnitude, relationships between figures and forms, and relations between quantities expressed symbolically. Math as we use it is the addition or subtraction people associate with investment gains or loses.

Money on the other hand can be measured by what's in your pockets, bank, or investments accounts. In other words, how much money do you have? People think math is how money works. Money is not math. It doesn't work like that.

Money is a commodity. It only has value when it is put into motion. Money can depreciate. Money can change. Money is Taxed. Money has gains and losses. Money has inflation, deflation and Valuations. Money is a moving target! People are using math to plan their financial futures because they view the concept of money and associate it with math. Many in the financial services industry like to refer to the average returns of a stock or investment portfolio has earned over a period of 5, 10, 20+ years. I often hear these advisors say, my account has averaged 10% over the past 10 years. I would like to ask them the question…." Have you ever done the "Math" on that? Here is an example on why Math is not money and Money is not math. Let's say you had a $100 in your investment account in 2017 and for the purpose of this example, the stock market declined 50% and you lose half the money in your account. Your $100 is now reduced to $50. You become irate! You call your broker to get guidance and direction. You ask your advisor, "How can this happen" and was given an appropriate answer. The Trade war with China, slowing of the economy, and dysfunction in the government were to blame. You take a deep breath, calm down and become encouraged after your advisor discusses your next moves. He comments, stocks are low. We will buy low and sell high. You are convinced that this strategy is where all real wealth takes place in the stock market. You are re-assured that the stock market would make a comeback and you adjust your asset allocations accordingly. The market rebounds in 2018 and gains 50% due to the new tax breaks given by the government administration and the increase of stock market prices due to corporation buying back their stock in large amounts after the corporate tax rate is reduced. You have a big ole smile on your face because your $50 had a 50% return. Don't believe the hype because now, it's time to do the math! You started with $100, lose 50% which reduced your account to $50 and had a 50% gain on the $50 which is a $25 gain and thus increased your balance in your investment account to $75. You had a 50% loss in one year and a 50% gain in year two, but you still lost $25 in value. People think that if they lose 50% and gain 50% that they'll be even but the math is, they'll lose 25% of their account! In order to break even in the stock market in year two, you would have to have a 100% gain. Math is not Money and Money is not Math.

- **Money Myth #7: Buy term life insurance and invest the difference.** Skip the expensive whole life insurance policies, buy term insurance, and invest the difference in the stock market through mutual funds was a popular marketing term certain insurance companies pushed into the marketplace to sell this over hyped philosophy. Buy term insurance and invest in the stock market and you will make so much money that you can "self-insure," meaning you will have enough cash in your investment accounts to replace income for your loved ones and thus will have no need for life insurance. You won't need any life insurance when you retire, the notion being that owning whole life cash value life insurance is something that only fools would do. The so-called "money experts" said, "Buy term insurance and use the difference you would have paid for the whole life and invest it in the stock market, and you will earn 10% per year or more. They say this is the best strategy to help secure your retirement.

Who needs life insurance in your retirement years?" This was, and still is, the shouting and talking points this crowd of people who have popular radio and television programs. This marketing strategy has misguided the public and I believe has led to much confusion for the public. I know, investing in the stock market is exciting, but most people who buy term and invest the difference not only don't invest the difference, they spend it! Often, they end up in the later years of their lives paying higher insurance premiums because they wake up at age 50 or older with their term insurance expiring with the same need for life insurance. I often get these types of calls…." My term insurance is expiring, I didn't invest the difference and my premiums are about to increase and I can't afford those higher premiums". If you are adopting this financial strategy you are being played! I will repeat…. you are being played! Another reason buying term insurance and investing the difference is a losing strategy is because most people buy term insurance and NEVER invest the difference! This leads to having no insurance and no retirement money to enjoy in your latter years of life. It is unfortunate that the stigma associated with insurance is so bad. I like to refer to this as the "eat less and exercise more to lose weight" strategy. These term insurance companies are doing a great job marketing and promoting this bad strategy. The insurance companies push these term life products because they make more profit selling these term policies over permanent life insurance policies. I get it! We live in a capitalist society, so the corporations must do whatever they can legally to make the most money. "Buy term and invest the difference" is a losing strategy. I feel that cash value life insurance is the greatest financial vehicle on the planet. I am a compassionate capitalist. I am going to share with you the benefits of owning permanent life insurance and utilizing the cash value and the cash value accumulation to build, develop, grow and protect your money and your legacy! Since the King is the most important piece on the chess board, cash value life insurance should be your most treasured asset in building and growing your financial empire!

Don't let these common myths stunt your financial success and keep you from building wealth. There's so much money advice out there that it can be difficult to differentiate the good ones from the bad ones, and this presents a serious problem. This is a serious problem because the mismanagement of money has caused people to lose access on interest, benefits, and taxes, which puts additional pressure on how their money is used. This book will give you a practical way to eliminate the noise and build a financial foundation centered on controlling the flow of money that comes under your management, reducing risk, eliminating fees, having money available to enjoy and repeat. While I transform your attitude and introduce some new beliefs, I think its first important to answer the question... "What should my money be doing for me?"

What should money be doing for you?

1. The first thing your money should be doing for you is to protect you. In order for your money to protect you, you have to protect IT. I am a big fan of Warren Buffet is who

considered to be one of the best minds in the financial services industry and is one of the richest men n the world. Warren Buffet's strategy is to stockpile large sums of cash to take advantage of opportunities. When the market drops, he buys depressed assets very cheaply. Warren Buffet believes it's a sin to lose to money. As a matter of fact, his number one golden rule is to never lose money. His second golden rule is to never forget rule number one.

Warren Buffet is more concerned about losing money instead of making gains. Loses affect your money because when you lose money, you give up the rights to earn interest on that money. Your future earnings potential on that money is gone forever!

2. Your money should be earning uninterrupted compound interest.

So, what is uninterrupted compound interest you may ask? Uninterrupted compound interest is a strategy in which you put your money in a vehicle that pays interest. At the end of the year, you take the interest earned add it to the principle and repeat the following year. The next year the principle and interest earned from the previous year is added to the new interest earned. The process repeats itself over and over. The longer the compounding interest grows uninterrupted the better it gets. The longer you allow your money to compound uninterrupted, the more it grows. The only factors that can stop the compounding from growing uninterrupted are taxes and fees so avoid them at all cost.

3. The third thing your money should do for you is to grow your nest egg. If you have accumulated healthy cash, you can use these funds in a variety of ways as an asset in your retirement portfolio. You can use these accumulated funds for lifestyle, retirement, purchase other assts, or store for further opportunities.

Common money mistakes everyday people make

Many of the prospective clients that seek help from me at Moore Financial Solutions have the same recurring money issues. Giving up control of their money is by far the biggest mistake people are making because once control is given up, so are access, flexibility, options, and growth. We have been conditioned to believe that money is not important because most of us have not had access to having money or building it. When you understand what's going on, you will know what to do. My job is to get you to understand what money mistakes you are making.

- **Money Mistake #1: Not investing in you!** You are your biggest investment. Personal development is the biggest money mistake people make when evaluating their finances. Take that course, get into a mastermind, attend that conference and get around creative people. If you don't make a plan and an investment in yourself to get better in your mindset, talent development, and skill set - you will remain poor. I am not just talking about money. You only need one great idea to become a millionaire.

- **Money Mistakes #2: Paying yourself last.** This is one of the cardinal sins of money management. You might be tempted to be a good steward by paying all of your bills first and then try to save afterwards. If you do this, don't be surprised to discover there is nothing left to put in the bank after all the bills have been paid. The tendency is to go to happy hour, spend money with friends, go out to dinner, or go on a shopping spree after all the household bills have been paid. Pay yourself first by having an automatic draft from your paycheck into a separate savings account with no debit card. If you don't see it, you're less likely to spend it.

- **Money Mistake #3: Having bad credit.** Having bad credit affects your ability to obtain a loan. Credit scores indicate the likelihood that you will default on a credit card or loan obligation. Having a low credit score means you are a high risk to repay the loan and thus assessed with higher interest rates. Having bad credit also affects your automobile and home insurances policies because low credit scores indicates to the insurance companies that you are a higher risk to default on your current obligations. Finally, having bad credit can affect your approval process for employment and or prohibit you from getting a job promotion or raise. How many times have you had to make a large down payment to move into an apartment, put a security deposit down on utilities (electric, phone, or cable) to obtain services? The biggest money mistake is buying a car with bad credit. If a lender approves you with a bad credit score, rest assured they will make you pay more interest and have a higher repayment monthly note, which will further destroy your ability to get control of your money.

- **Money Mistake #4: Carrying high interest credit card debt.**

  High interest credit card debt is easy to get into and hard to get out of it because it robs you by making payments that you could have been earning interest on. It can be one purchase or one series of purchases that gets you into large credit card debt. A Starbucks here, a Starbucks there, A dinner here, vacation trip there, meeting friends for drinks, splurging on a shopping trip, and before you know it the minimum payment on credit card balances takes a significant chunk of your paycheck. Then the interest charges add up, further crippling your ability to save toward your goals.

Credit card companies will give you the opportunity to pay back this debt over time but having a high credit card balance is bad for you for the following reasons:

a) *High credit card balances hurt your credit score.* According to Experian, high credit card balance can affect your credit score up to 45 points or more per card. When the balance on your credit card balance exceeds 30% of your credit limit, it negatively affects your overall score.

b) *Higher credit card balances increase your monthly repayment amount.* Have you noticed how high your monthly credit card bill is? The bigger the balance, the higher the monthly bill.

c) *You're at a higher risk of being in debt.* Debt happens when you repeatedly borrow more money than you are able to pay back. Having a high credit card balance, especially on more than one credit card, doesn't help your debt situation and keeps you trapped in making bad financial decisions.

- **Money Mistake #5: Spending too much money on housing.**

  How many of you have heard the old adage "House rich, dollar poor?" If you haven't, it means your house payment is a considerably higher monthly obligation than what your monthly budget can afford. This happens when you exceed the recommended percentage of 30% of your monthly income for the purchase and maintenance of your home or the rental of your apartment. Money is something that probably affects everything you do. You might work for it, worry about it, spend some of it, and even wish you had more of it.

- **Money Mistake #6 Living in a culture of debt.**

  America loves money, America loves debt, and America loves consumerism. As a result, just like with the money myths, we've noticed some common mistakes among people of all income levels that could be hurting their ability to manage their day-to-day finances and save for their longer-term goals. Debt levels are high, and savings levels are low.

Every day, millions of individuals go to work feeling the strain caused by bad financial decisions. It seems that one of the biggest problems many people are struggling with is basic money management skills. The lack of basic money management skills cripples your ability to protect yourself and your family against financial setbacks. According to a 2017 study conducted by Bankrate.com, people are stressed about money and are barely making ends meet. In fact, nearly 60 percent of Americans don't have enough cash on hand to cover a $500 expense. Americans are making this mistake because they fail to save money first before spending. You can't save if you spend everything you earn. We all make mistakes with money, so it's important that we develop a game plan. We must have a mindset that we are going to win with money each day, week, month and year. When you have no game plan and your mind is not renewed, you will stay in a pattern where you spend everything you make because you are not paying attention to your money and thus asking for financial trouble.

- **Money Mistake #7 Not understanding the tax code**

  Americans are not using the tax code properly to plan for financial success. One of the biggest tax mistakes Americans are making each year is getting a tax refund. According to IRS data, the IRS issued approximately $464 billion in tax refunds in 2018. While a refund may seem exciting, it's just your own money coming back to you after a year of earning you no interest and having no access to the funds. You work hard for your money and you should be able to make the most of it. Giving an interest-free loan to the IRS doesn't allow you to do that. What I want you to realize is that you did not earn any interest on this money. This money was not available for you in case of emergencies and if you wanted it to invest, you'll have missed out on the returns you could've earned during the time the Internal Revenue Service had your money. We call this lost opportunity cost. To make sure you don't end up getting a big income tax refund next year, consider adjusting your withholding with your employer by updating your W-4 form so the correct amount is withheld from your paycheck. Ideally, you should have just enough withheld from your paychecks to break even at the end of the year. This will also increase your take home pay. Another mistake Americans make is missing tax deadlines. It might seem unbelievable but sending in your tax returns late is one of the biggest mistakes' taxpayers make. Many people wait until the last minute to submit their returns and don't complete their taxes in time before the 11:59 p.m. deadline on April 15th and end up paying penalties to the I.R.S. because of it. It's always a good idea to give yourself more time than you think you'll need to file, just in case any last-minute issues come up. If you send your return by mail, send your documents certified mail with registered receipt requested. If you are a 1099 worker, freelancer, or business owner, you especially need to pay attention to important tax deadlines throughout the year. The biggest mistake I see in this area is people failing to make estimated income tax payments and then getting assessed the failure to pay and sometimes even failure to file penalties by both the I.R.S and their state taxing authority. The fines and fees are excessive. The good news is these penalties can be waived for certain taxpayers who owe less than $1,000 in taxes after subtracting their withholdings and credits, or those who paid at least 90% of the tax owed for the current year or 100% of the tax shown on the return for the prior year, whichever is smaller. Another error is not understanding where the biggest deductions are in in U.S. tax code. The tax code is a series of incentives the government gives for the landowner and the business owner. The government wants you to do certain things with your money to help stimulate the economy. These tax incentives basically tell you what to do to maximize your money. The two biggest tax incentives are in real estate and business ownership. Save your money and get into the game. Investigate and find yourself a good tax advisor to investigate how you can take advantage of these incentives. The final mistake is paying into tax deferred accounts. Paying into tax deferred accounts is when you withheld paying current taxes now and delay paying taxes in the future by saving into a 401(k), IRA, 403(b), or 457 plan. I often wonder why anyone would defer taxes into the future when taxes are now historically low? When you defer taxes on your money, what you are doing is telling the government that you will pay the taxes at a later time, at age 59 1/2 or later. The government mandates you to start withdrawing money at age 72 because it wants to start receiving tax revenue on the money you deferred. The government allows you to do this, because mathematically they know they will collect more tax revenue in the future, especially when death occurs. This philosophy is old and outdated. To give you some historical perspective of these programs, we have to travel back to the year 1978. Congress passed the Revenue Act of 1978, which included a provision that was added to the Internal Revenue Code — Section 401(k) — that allowed employees to avoid being taxed on deferred compensation. Despite their popularity today, these tax deferred programs (401(k), IRA, 403(b), etc.) were created almost by accident. Ted Benna, also known as the father of the 401(k) plan, petitioned the I.R.S to modify Section 401(k), which was written as part of the Revenue Act, and in 1981 the I.R.S complied. Participants in 401(k) plans could then use their deferred income to make investments without being taxed on gains. The 401(k) plan was also used to give the employee an incentive to save for retirement, and some corporations exchanged the idea of having a pension plan for a 401(k) plan with a company match. The top income bracket in 1981 was 70% on $107,000 of income or more for a married couple and $108,000 if you were single. The idea of deferring taxes to make investments without being taxed made perfect sense. Corporations and financial institutions sold this idea to the employees and thus the 401(k) plan for retirement took off. Deferring paying taxes now on money going into your retirement and paying the taxes later was a good idea. Taxes were high, and the thought of deferring taxes into the future because at retirement time you would be in a lower tax bracket was appealing. The banking and financial institutions marketed these products to encourage you to give them your money so they could earn fees and transfer the risk to you. In today's tax environment, taxes are very low. Do you think taxes will be higher in the future? By deferring taxes (not paying taxes on money now) and delaying paying into the future could be more costly. The top income bracket today is 37% set to increase to 39.6% in 2025. Some believe taxes could return to the top tax bracket of 70% or more because of ever-increasing government debt. At retirement time you are given three tax deductions (home, kids, business) and the current government debt is over twenty-four trillion dollars and growing, according to usdebtclock.org. If taxes rise even higher to pay the outstanding government debt your 401k or other tax-deferred retirement plan can be taxed even higher. If you are in a lower tax bracket in retirement than the rates today, that means you were a complete financial failure! Is it your goal to save money into the future to end up being a complete financial failure at retirement? Under our current tax system, that's the only way you would win. I recommend paying the tax now while taxes are historically low and put your money into accounts where it can never be taxed again because taxes will be going up.

- **Money Mistake #8 Not leaving money for the next generation**. The final money mistake many people are making is not planning for a financial legacy. The effects of not leaving a financial legacy for the future cripples the money for the next generation to have opportunities to develop their dreams, talents and goals. Life has to end one day, and you have to consider leaving behind money for your children, grandchildren, church or charity. Leaving a legacy means putting a stamp on the future and making a contribution for future generational success. Leaving a legacy is a way to let others appreciate our love and our consideration for them because we took the time to plan ahead for the impact our absence would have on them. Building a secure financial future and legacy for your family doesn't happen accidentally. It takes discipline, money, consistency, effort, and focus. Is this the reason why more people are not leaving a financial legacy for the next generation? If so, my goal is to interrupt your current pattern of how you are reviewing your money so you can regain your money freedom and reach new levels of financial success.

My goal is to help you gain control over the flow of your money, create tax free income at retirement and leave a financial legacy for the next generation to enjoy and repeat. Here at Moore Financial Solutions, we have recently developed a 10/10/10/50/20 rule of thumb that can be used as a starting point for building wealth, spending this wealth, and leaving a legacy for the next generation. Consider the following guidelines for saving and budgeting:

- 10% Tithe to Church or favorite charity

- 10% "what if "account for emergencies

- 10% of take-home pay into a specially designed cash value life insurance policy
- 50% necessities (housing, medical care, debt payments, transportation and food)

- 20% lifestyle expenses (travel, dining out, shopping, entertainment)

When the 10% emergency account is completed, take that 10% and put it into an opportunities account to build passive income or start a business. Follow this guideline to develop good money habits and help position you to live an awesome lifestyle. It is always a good idea to develop a detailed understanding of where your money is going. It all starts with a plan and having the will power, continued knowledge and tenacity to see the program through. We also need to take a page from the banking institutions who are the masters with money. In order to get a better viewpoint on how banks make money we have to see how banks lure customers in to give them money. Banks grow by paying their customers to lend them money. The depositing account holder gains a small amount of money in return (interest on savings), and the lending customer pays a larger amount of money to the bank in return (interest on loans). To make money for itself, the bank keeps the difference. Banks have also mastered a principle called the "velocity of money".

Velocity of money is a measure of how fast money passes from one holder to the next. It is most commonly measured as the speed at which money is used to purchase goods and services within a given time period. In other words, take a dollar, spend a dollar, get the same dollar back to spend it again. I like to refer to it as how the banks make money since the banking industry is the only industry that doesn't produce a product or good. Banks make money using this principle of velocity to get your money, lending it back out in the form of loans, and getting your money back again to relend it out again. Banks continually repeat this process. Most good banks can do this effectively with one dollar in and relend that dollar out again 30+ times before that one dollar becomes void.

I want you to understand how the banks dominate this principle. To understand how the banks are killing it with the velocity of money concept, you must understand that banks want your money! Your money is the key to making this velocity of money system work for them. Banks want your money on a systematic basic. They want to make sure you keep giving your money to them every payday, so much so that banks will give you incentives, (i.e., won't charge you any fees to have your money directly deposited into their accounts) to receive your money on a systematic basis. Banks want to hold onto your money as long as possible because as long as they can hold onto it, they can make more!

Banks are masters in capturing and controlling your money. If you are not controlling this concept in your life, then you are making the wheels on the banking system turn. The system is designed for you to focus on rate of return and not on the control and flow of money. Banks have mastered the velocity of money concept and are getting PAID! That's why they can have naming rights on most big sporting or entertainment venues. They have developed complex programs to get you to send them money on a regular basis. You don't have to be rich to get into the banking business. You can create an entity that mirrors the banking functions in your life. Everything is being done to condition the way you think, so the question is, "What if you could take what the banks are doing with velocity of money and do it for yourself?" It is my belief that the insurance companies were the first the introduce this concept of velocity of money and profit from it. It is also my belief that the insurance executives who ran the insurance companies understood this concept and worked it so well that they left the insurance industry and started banks as we know them today. This concept of velocity of money is so strong that once you understand how to get maximum turns on the same dollar you can grow your financial portfolio, and more importantly, keep control of your money yourself. What I find remarkably interesting is that banks do not follow their own rules when it comes to investing their own money. Banks don't put their cash into mutual funds, stocks, hedge funds, term life insurance, or risky real estate deals. Since banks are only required to keep the minimum money on hand required by law, usually 3-10% of their total daily transactions, and this fluctuates during the holidays. Where do banks put their excess capital or reserves?

The top banking institutions in America place a large portion of their assets and cash reserves into high cash value life insurance policies known as Bank Owned Life Insurance (BOLI). Bank-Owned Life Insurance is a tax efficient method that offsets employee benefit costs. The bank purchases and owns an insurance policy on an executive's life and is the beneficiary. Cash values grow tax-deferred providing the bank with monthly bookable income. The banks obtain uninterrupted compound interest, guaranteed interest rates and access to cash within the cash value account; and upon the executive's death a tax-free death benefit is paid to the bank. BOLI is used as a tax efficient method for offsetting the costs of employee benefit programs. Historically, BOLI was often combined with a new executive benefit plan for senior executives. However, in more recent years many banks have added BOLI in order to offset existing employee benefit expenses. Top banks in America have invested and accumulated billions of dollars into high cash value life insurance. What do the banks know about cash value life insurance that many of your favorite financial advisors don't know? The amounts banks have invested into life insurance companies is large, and quickly growing. Why is cash value life insurance for many banks their largest asset class? According to the FDIC website, almost 3800 banks own over $190 billion dollars in cash value in Bank Owned Life Insurance policies. Bank of America owns $22 billion, Wells Fargo owns $18 billion and JP Morgan Chase owns $11 billion in cash value assets as per their 2019 third quarter balance sheet. If cash value life insurance is such a bad investment, why do banks own more cash value life insurance than all of their real estate, stocks, bonds and mutual funds combined? After all, isn't the banking industry doing exactly what television and radio show mega authors warn consumers NOT to do? What do the banks know about cash value life insurance that you don't? The banking industry gets many benefits from buying billions of dollars in cash value life insurance and we will discuss the top five benefits.

- **Benefit #1 - Competitive Return**. Steady return year after year with no risk. Superior returns than what the bank can typically offer.

- **Benefit #2 – Tax Deferred Growth**. No taxes paid on accumulation, so compound interest gets the opportunity to grow the money.

- **Benefit #3 – Liquidity and Accessibility**. Money is easily accessible and can be used to purchase other assets like real estate, stocks, bonds, etc. This money can be used for any reason and for any purpose.

- **Benefit #4 – Unlimited Contributions** – No restrictions on how much money can go into the programs.

- **Benefit #5 – Death Benefit** – Death benefits are paid income tax free.

Banks love cash value life insurance because when structured properly, banks know they can't lose any money and will get a higher interest rate of return on their money from cash value growth than they can get at their own bank! Many banks often choose to make cash value a significant percentage of their "top-tier" capital and rely on it as a means to withstand financial instability. The banks also know that unlike investments there are no carrying costs, fees, and they can surrender the plan without any surrender charges. The trick to building wealth is to do what the banking, financial institutions, and their executives are DOING, not what they TELL investors to do. Maybe it's time to un-plug yourself from how you've been programmed to act and invest. Maybe it's time to re-examine your assumptions and take advantage of one of the most powerful financial products called cash value life insurance! Cash value life insurance is a form of permanent life insurance that features a cash value savings component. The cash value earns a modest rate of interest with a minimum guaranteed interest rate, grows taxes deferred on the accumulated earnings, and is paid out income tax free at death.

Section 3

What is Life insurance and how does it work?

This section is dedicated to explaining life insurance in a nutshell. As I write this chapter, I think of all the people who didn't have access to cash value life insurance and to all of the people who were trained that insurance is a death only product. It is my goal to take the confusion out of life insurance. You must understand the differences because the insurance companies would love to keep you confused about these products because where there is confusion, there is PROFIT, and lots of it!!! Life insurance as we are using it today is being used primarily to bury our love ones at death. People miss out on the greatest benefits life insurance affords because most see it as a death only product. Many are under the misperception that life insurance is expensive, contains little benefits, and is an overall bad investment. According to the Life Insurance Marketing and Research Association (LIMRA), only 59 percent of Americans have life insurance, and about half of those with insurance are underinsured. Many only have coverage at work and are unaware of the biggest benefits that cash value life insurance affords. If life insurance's biggest attribute was for death, they would have named it death insurance, yet the name implies that its greatest asset is in the living components. Cash value life insurance is a form of permanent life insurance that features a cash value savings component. The policyholder can use the cash value for many purposes, such as a source of loans, as a source of cash, or to pay policy premiums. Advantages such as tax-free accumulation, tax-free distributions, liability suit protection, paycheck replacement, guaranteed uninterrupted compound interest, and having the ability to build an asset to use to buy other investments is how cash value life insurance should be marketed and promoted to families to protect their money and legacy. My goal is to get you to understand how cash value life insurance can be a valuable asset for your overall financial game plan. If I can get you to understand what's going on, I believe you will know what to do. The key players in life insurance are the owner of the policy, the company, the insured and the beneficiary. The owner in most cases is the insured (the person who is covered) but can also be anyone who has an insurable interest in the insured. (e.g. your mother, father, husband, wife or company etc.) The policy is a legal contract between the owner of the policy and the life insurance company. The insurance company pays out a lump sum death benefit to the beneficiary of the policy upon the death of the insured. There are mutual life insurance companies, whereas the policyholder participates in the profitability, skills and risk associated with the insurance company earning a profit. The insurance company will reward or share in their profits with its policyholders in the form of a dividend to the cash value, which are a return of premiums and not income, therefore the dividend when declared will increase the cash value and death benefit and not be subject to income tax if structured the proper way. Stock insurance companies share their profits with their stockholders, who are nonparticipating and receive no dividend. I am not a big fan of stock insurance companies because stock companies pay no dividends. Nearly all the profits stock insurance companies make are distributed to the stockowners and little if anything is left over for the insured to benefit from in the form of increased cash value or death benefit. I am a big fan of mutual life insurance companies because dividends matter! Life insurance companies collect information that determines the risk the insurance companies would take. Such information as age, gender, health, occupation, driving history, hobbies, drug or nicotine use factors into the cost the insurance company will take to insure the risk. We know this as premiums you pay to cover the risk. There are no deals in the life insurance industry. Everything is a tradeoff between cost and risk. You will either have lower cost with lower risk or higher cost with higher risk. There are three main types of life insurance: Term, Universal, and Permanent or Whole Life insurance. Actuarially, there are three basic pricing assumptions that go into every type of life insurance:

Mortality-- How many individuals will die each year using a large sample size—i.e. the 1980 CSO Mortality Table or the newer 2001 CSO Mortality Table. Most life insurance companies use their own proprietary mortality experience based on their own internal set of statistics. The CSO Mortality Tables reflect total population figures within the US and do not reflect how a life insurance company screens its applicants for good health during the policy underwriting phase of the policy issue process. Corporate mortality will most likely always be more favorable than CSO tables as a result. In rare cases, some companies have recently increased policy mortality costs on existing business segments due to much lower than anticipated investment returns. Assumed Net Investment Return, i.e. current industry average return of 5.5% annual yield by the life insurance company. In the early 1980's interest/return assumptions were well over 10% to be sustained over the life of the policy.

Internal Administrative Expenses-- Generally these are proprietary figures which include policy acquisition costs (sales commissions to selling agents and brokers) and general home office expenses. There are three types of life insurance and it's important to know the difference because all life insurance is not created equally.

Term insurance is basically a type of life insurance contract whereby the insurance company provides coverage for a certain number of years. The company offers death protection insurance at a fixed rate of payment for a limited, specific period. If you die within the time period defined in the terms, the insurance company will pay your beneficiaries the face value of your policy. Term insurance is a clear example of lower cost and lower risk. The premium/cost is so cheap because most people outlive the term. The risk to the insurance company to pay the death benefit on a term insurance contract is very low because you assume all the risk! This is why the cost is so cheap. According to a study conducted by Penn State University, 99% of all term policies written in America never paid a claim.! What should you know about term insurance? Term insurance is basically a type of life insurance contract whereby the insurance company provides coverage for a certain number of years. The company offers death protection insurance at a fixed rate of payment for a limited, specific period. If you die within the time period defined in the terms, the insurance company will pay your beneficiaries the face value of your policy. The policy owner pays a specific and defined amount of money for a specific amount of death benefit. For example, you have 500,000 worth of life insurance coverage for a 20-year period. If you die within the 20 years, the insurance company will pay the 500,000 to your named beneficiary. If you die the 20th year plus one day after the policy expired, the insurance company will pay no benefit to your family. The insurance coverage ceases when the term expires. All of the money you spent ends up in their pockets and a benefit to your family is never paid out. Life insurance companies price the term insurance to be cheap in the early years and more expensive in the later years. They also price the term insurance to be cheaper than Whole Life insurance because they know after the term insurance expires, the premium increase will be too costly for you to keep.

- **Yearly Renewable Term Insurance:**

  This term contract gives you one year's worth of insurance protection for a set premium which does not change for the entire year. Yearly renewable term is also known as Annual Renewable Term, which is a short-term life insurance policy that can be renewed every year for a defined length of time. When the policy is renewed each year, the premiums go up, increasing more and more the older you get. Annual renewable term is the cheapest way to purchase your life insurance.

- **Level Premium Term Policies:**

Level premium policies have the benefit of level premiums for an extended period. When you purchase the policy, you choose the number of years you want to keep the term insurance in force. You have 10, 15, 20, 30-year level term periods. In this type of insurance plan, the premium paid each year remains the same for the duration of the contract. This cost is based on the summary cost of each year's annual renewable term rates, with a time value of money adjustment made by the insurer. Thus, the longer the term period which the premium remains the same, the higher the premium amount. The excess premium collected is invested in the insurance company's general investment account. In the later years of the policy, this excess premium, plus investment interest, is used to hold down the rising cost of the insurance, thus keeping the premium level for the selected (10,15,20,30 year) duration of the contract term. The premiums will be higher each year for longer term policies.

- **Return of Premium Term Life Insurance**

  Term life insurance coverage that provides a return of all the premiums paid during the policy term if the insured person outlives the duration of the term life insurance policy. For example, if an individual owns a 20-year return of premium term life insurance plan and the 20-year term has expired, the premiums paid by the owner will be returned, less any fees and expenses which the life insurance company incurred. Usually, a return of premium policy returns almost all the premiums paid by the insured if he/she outlives the policy term. The premiums for a return premium term life plan are usually much higher than for a regular level term life insurance policy since the insurer needs to make money by using the premiums as an interest free loan, rather than as a non-returnable premium.

- **Decreasing Term Life Insurance**

This is one type of insurance I would never buy, but since I am in the education business, I am obligated to tell you what it means even though I would never buy it personally or recommend it to anyone! Decreasing term insurance is designed to pay a lower death benefit as the policy ages. The death benefit decreases in value throughout the period of the plan. This reduction is typically a monthly decrease. While this type of coverage may at first sound odd, it is primarily sold to insure people who currently have mortgage loans or other large debts.

- **Convertible Term Life Insurance**

  Convertible term policy allows the insured to convert a term policy into a permanent policy later. If the conditions of the policy have been maintained and payments made on time, the insured person is not required to undergo any new underwriting criteria or additional screening at the time the policy is converted, regardless of his/her medical condition. This type of policy provides the benefit of obtaining less expensive term life insurance now while maintaining the option to convert to a permanent policy later as insurance needs and financial resources change. In plain English, convertible term insurance allows you to convert a term policy to a permanent life insurance policy and have coverage for the rest of your life, even if your health deteriorates and you become "uninsurable" since getting your first policy. Term insurance is a lot like renting an apartment. No matter how many years or decades you pay rent, you get no credit for prior payments if you can't pay this month's rent. You have a landlord, which in this case is the insurance company. You pay your landlord each month and you obtain no equity in the property. The landlord can change the rules at any time. You have no control over your policy, no ownership interest, and your rent will be lower in the beginning, but higher over the long run compared to paying a mortgage on your home. You get limited tax benefits and you have no flexibility. There are limited choices for how long your coverage lasts until the policy is converted to permanent coverage. If you stop paying your premium, the insurance company will cancel your coverage in 31 days. With term insurance, the only benefit the family will have is if the insured dies during the term period. I want to also note that term is a great short-term strategy to obtain insurability, but it's a horrible long-term strategy because the insurance company will make all the money and receive all the benefits. The insurance companies take the insurance premium, the interest it made on the insurance premiums, and it gets the death benefit back when the term expires! It is a cash cow for the insurance companies, thus why they make the premiums so low! Insurance companies love to underwrite term policies with limited conversion options because it wants to keep 99% of the profits after the term expires. Always remember, term insurance has an expiration date. If you can qualify for the coverage, the insurance company knows you will outlive the expiration date! The pricing goal for the insurance company is to get you to pay premiums for 10, 20, 30 years, have you outlive the coverage, get all the premiums for the stated term years, and more importantly get the death benefit back after you cancel the policy because the premiums increases. Many insurance companies offer cheap term-only policies and make a killing because people simply outlive the term of the contract, so the beneficiary never collects the death benefit. Sweet deal for the insurance companies! Only buy term insurance that is convertible and be sure to convert it into a permanent plan within the first seven years. Ten years maximum.

Universal Life Insurance

Universal life insurance is a type of flexible permanent life insurance contract that offers low-cost protection of term insurance as well as a savings element, which is invested to provide cash value if the savings element generates positive returns. The term insurance costs increase in the contract each year. Insurance companies developed universal life insurance back in the 1980's to be competitive with the stock market, CD's, bonds, and checking and savings accounts with interest rates being paid as high as 18%. Since the 1980's interest rates have progressively gone lower and many of those policies are no longer in force because the insurance costs are higher the older you get. Let me explain these types of policies. For the most part, they are designed to expire before you do. They are cash cows for the insurance companies because most of these policies will never pay out a claim. Any type of insurance programs with an increasing term cost provision - stay away! Let's dig deeper. Here is what should you know about universal life insurance. Universal life insurance is also known as adjustable or flexible payment life insurance. Policies vary radically from policy to policy and company to company. They can have price guarantees as low as only 3 years or as high as 60 years. There are some that, under certain conditions, will give a lifetime guarantee, but let's get to the basis of what Universal Life insurance is.

Universal Life insurance contains two different parts. Part one covers the cost of life insurance expenses which are one-year annual renewable term insurance costs and administrative fees. Part two goes into a savings or investment account which can carry additional fund management fees. The insured is protected with a guaranteed amount of death insurance protection and the excess money goes into the policy's savings component, which is saved in an interest-bearing account to provide the policy holder with cash value build up. This cash can grow on a tax deferred basis. The insurance cost will increase each year and you are banking on earning more interest in the savings component to offset the rising yearly term insurance and administrative costs. What happens to the contract if you can't pay the additional costs of insurance and fees in the latter years? The policy will expire and all the money you put into the policy will be gone. You have many investment choices for a universal life policy, and they will vary. In general, you may choose between an interest rate tied to current interest rates, investment returns derived from the insurer's separate account, or an equity-indexed investment strategy managed by the company. What makes universal life insurance different is the fact that premiums, cash values, and coverage limits may be increased or decreased during the lifetime of the policy. Universal Life is what I refer to as "fake whole life" because technically you can keep the policy in force for life but the increasing term insurance and administration expenses in the later years may kill you first because the costs will go up each year and eventually eat away all the cash in the policy. Universal life insurance works best if you plan to not get older each year.

Indexed Universal Life

Indexed Universal life insurance contains two different parts which the premiums pay for. Part one covers the cost of life insurance expenses which are one-year annual renewable term insurance cost and administrative fees. Part two can be guaranteed or non-guaranteed with an option to tie your return to a major stock market index like the S&P 500, Nasdaq 100, Russell 2000 or some other domestic/international stock market indexes. You are credited with an interest credit if the account goes up based on the investment performance inside of the index. The insurance costs increase each year and you are banking on earning more interest/money in the index account to offset the rising yearly insurance costs.

Variable Universal Life Insurance

Variable Universal life insurance contains two different parts which the insurance premiums pay for. Part one covers the cost of life insurance expenses which are one-year annual renewable term insurance costs, administrative fees and fund manager expenses. Part two is separately managed accounts, referred to as sub-accounts or mutual funds. You are credited with an interest credit if the mutual fund account goes up inside of the sub accounts. Your cash value and death benefit increase if the underlying investments do well, or they may shrink considerably under poor investment performance. The insurance costs increase each year and you are banking on earning more money in the sub accounts (mutual funds) to offset the rising yearly insurance costs. Universal/Variable life insurance is what I like to refer to as "fake whole life". Universal/Variable life insurance is a lot like owning a mobile home in a mobile home park. You have the opportunity to purchase the mobile home at a set price (insurance coverage) but you will rent the land it sits on from the mobile park owner, or in this case the insurance company. The insurance company will raise the rent on the land the mobile home sits on each year. Your mobile home will have the opportunity to increase in value each year through equity or in this case cash value and based on the land it sits on will increase in value. There are tax benefits like tax deferral cash accumulation, income tax free distributions through cash value appreciation, and income tax free distribution through life insurance death benefit pay out. The mobile home will enjoy many of the benefits of owning a permanent home but the key thing which destroys the value of the mobile home, or in this case the life insurance, is the rising costs of the rent that must be paid on the property each year to the mobile park owner, or in this case the insurance company. The insurance companies actuarially design these types of policies to expire before the person dies (policy fees and cost of insurance are most costly during your later years in life where you are closer to your death) and thus makes a big PROFIT! The Longer you pay rent on that mobile park (term insurance) the longer the mobile park owner (insurance company) makes money. The insurance companies love these types of policies because they get term insurance payments for a longer duration than an actual term policy (in most cases), additional administration fees, surrender charges if policy is surrendered and investment fees. The insurance companies are singing the "Best of Both Worlds" song because that's what they receive every time a Universal Life/Variable Life policy is sold, because they get the best of both worlds - insurance premiums and separate account/investment fees.

Whole Life Insurance

Whole Life insurance is the most common type of life insurance. It guarantees payment of a death benefit to beneficiaries in exchange for level, regularly due premium payments. Premiums are level as you live, and your policy builds cash value. The initial annual cost will be much higher than the same amount of term life insurance. Whole life insurance is often called "expensive" because the insurance company assumes more risk. Insurance companies guarantee they will pay the death benefit and its benefits whether one outlives the contract or not. The tradeoff is that there are higher costs because the insurance company is on the hook to perform as the contract states. Whole life insurance has a cash-value component in addition to a life insurance component. Premium payments are split between these two parts, leading to higher rates. Part one covers the cost of life insurance expenses which are fixed over the length of the policy, and administrative expenses. The second part of the policy includes a savings portion, called the cash value. When considering a whole life insurance policy, only purchase a policy that will pay a dividend. We call this Participating Whole Life Insurance because the insurance company participates in helping you earn money! In other words, the insurance company shares its profits with its policy holders! Dividend paying whole life insurance is the best form of whole life insurance you can and should buy. Here's why: The dividend, when declared will increase the cash value and more importantly increase the life insurance death benefit. The dividend once declared can never be taken back. The cash value will accumulate on a tax-deferred basis. Growing cash value is an essential component of whole life insurance. When a "super charger" Paid-up Additions rider is added on to the insurance policy, policyholders get the opportunity to increase their living benefit and death benefit by increasing the policy's cash value. The Paid-up Additions portion themselves will also earn dividends, and the value continues to compound indefinitely over time. Whole life policies build up cash value slowly at first, but then will pick up the pace after several years when your cash value starts to grow faster than your insurance cost and administrative fees. At this point, the magic will start to happen because the insurance company will start to put more money in your cash value account than you are paying in premiums. We affectionately refer to this as "the breakpoint or crossover." At some point, the cash value will grow to the point that it could be used to continue to pay for your insurance premiums, buy other investments or generate tax free income for life. The longer you have whole life insurance, the better the cash value gets because of its compounding effect.

Single premium whole life insurance

Single premium whole life is a life insurance policy that is paid up after one large initial payment. The policy will continue to increase in value each year because the policy will have guaranteed cash value plus interest. If the company declares a dividend, the dividend will help the cash value and death benefit increase in value.

Limited payment whole life insurance

Limited payment whole life insurance is a life insurance policy that lets you pay premiums for only a specific period. This time period can be 10 years, 20 years or until age 65. You will pay premiums for this time duration and your life insurance will be paid for the rest of your life. After payment, your policy will continue to earn dividends as declared and your cash value will continue to grow. As a result, premium payments will be higher than if payments were spread out through your lifetime. Whole life insurance is a lot like owning a home. The premium payments are more costly in the beginning but cheaper over the years just like owning a home is cheaper than renting an apartment over the long term. Whole life insurance, just like the name implies, is life insurance coverage for your entire life. What is the chance you will die in this lifetime? 100 %, so whole life insurance guarantees that benefits and replacement of income will be there for your named beneficiary. Whole life insurance is a lot like owning a home because your premiums are predictable and more stable than renting because rent rates go up each year while whole life insurance premiums stay the same. Just like owning a home, the whole life policy will build equity that the homeowner can use for whatever reason. Whole life insurance also has favorable tax treatment. Money that accumulates in the whole life policy grows tax deferred and can be taken out income tax free without a penalty. The whole life insurance death benefit is also paid out income tax free. Home ownership has an instant pride factor which helps to build your ego and whole life insurance gives that same feeling. There is nothing like the feeling of owning something that no one can take away from you! From the title of this book, you know I am a big believer in cash value life insurance and permanent life insurance as the best way to own your insurance. Cash value life insurance is also a threat to the banking institutions. The banks do not want you to know of the benefits of cash value life insurance because you can set your financial life up to provide the same functions as the banks and the banks wouldn't like that because you would be eating into their profits!!! A super charged, specially designed cash value life insurance contract will provide you access to your money when you need it! Unlike a regular savings account, 401(k), 403(b), mutual funds, or IRA account, this super charged cash value life insurance policy is backed by the amount of money you put in it. You can access this cash at any time for any reason while still earning compound interest! You can borrow up to 85% of your total cash value in your account. You can use this cash value to pay off high interest credit card debt, purchase real estate investment property, create a retirement income, buy or invest in a business, purchase stocks, take a vacation or do whatever your heart desires! The original amount in your supercharged cash value account will continue to grow and earn a tax-free return ranging anywhere from 3-5%. All you have to do is pay back the loan plus interest that is paid back to your account minus a small percentage and repeat the process. If you are not able to pay back the loan, the loan plus interest will be paid off at death with the increasing death benefit. Can you see how a supercharged, specially designed cash value life insurance contract can replace your bank? This information is the greatest threat to the banking industry, and they don't want you to know about it! The banking industry does not financially benefit from your cash value life insurance so there is virtually no advertising about it. This is the big secret the banks don't want you to know about because YOU are a threat to their earnings!

Many wealthy individuals have structured specially designed super charged cash value life insurance contracts in the past that have saved their businesses. Case in point, Walt Disney used his cash value to help fund Disneyland, his first theme park in 1953, when no banker would approve his loan. So many bankers rejected his idea of funding Disneyland because they thought his idea of a theme park focusing on kids was crazy. Walt Disney was able to access the funds needed through his cash value account to fund his dream of building this amusement park where parents and children could come together and have a good time. What was the return on that cash value investment? BIG!!! Another example where cash value was used where the banks said no to a loan was Ray Kroc of McDonalds. Kroc used his cash value life insurance as an emergency account to help save his businesses during difficult times. Kroc, one of the original owners of McDonalds, used his cash value to help meet payroll during difficult times when he first started McDonalds. As a young business owner, Kroc made very little money and reinvested what little gains he had back into the business. He did not take a salary during his first 8 years! He struggled and had many cash-flow problems. Ray Kroc eventually tapped into his cash value of his life insurance to save his business and to help cover the salaries of his key employees. He had a brilliant idea to create a mascot to help promote his business. Where did he get the money for this new mascot? You guessed it! He used the remaining cash value to create an advertising campaign around this new mascot which later emerged as the mascot we love today as Ronald McDonald! What could cash value do you for? Cash value also saved JC Penney after the stock market crash of 1929. JC Penney had accumulated over 1,400 stores across the country, and his stores were thriving before the stocks market crashed and burned and the "Great Depression" devasted his personal wealth and threatened to close all his stores. With his funds declining, Penney was able to use his cash value to meet the payroll and expenses, which allowed him to rebound. Having guaranteed growth with access to equity with no questions asked were powerful features that allowed JC Penney to pull his business out of the gutter, rebound, and make sales which today exceed $2 billion dollars. Cash value life insurance also saved Stanford University. Stanford was founded in 1885 by Leland and Jane Stanford in honor of their only child, Leland Stanford Jr., who had died of typhoid fever at age 15. Leland Stanford was a U.S. Senator and former Governor of California who made his fortune as a railroad tycoon. He and his wife Jane decided they would use their wealth to do something for other people's children through education to honor the life of their only child. They decided to build a university as the most fitting memorial and deeded to it a large fortune that included the 8,180-acre Palo Alto stock farm that became the campus. Leland Stanford Jr. University, which is still its original name, opened in Palo Alto California in 1891, with a pioneer class of 555 students, with the most notable student being former President Herbert Hoover. Leland Stanford died in 1893 and Stanford University struggled to keep its school open. Professors were not getting paid and Jane Stanford went as far as to try to sell her precious jewelry collection to save the school. That attempt failed and Stanford University was in danger of closing. Jane eventually used the proceeds from her husband's life insurance policy to help keep the school open by funding operations and paying the professors which allowed Stanford University to weather a dangerous six-year period of financial distress. Cash value helped Stanford secure its legacy as of one of the best universities in the nation, as well as protect the legacy of one of the top fundraising institutions in the country, as Stanford is the first school to raise more than a billion dollars in a year. Finally, cash value life insurance saved ME!!! 2008 and 2009 were the worse financial years of my life. In 2005, we upgraded our financial office and moved into a bigger office in Mount Laurel, NJ. My wife and I accumulated real estate investments and were debt free. I had a business line of credit and money in the bank! My wife and I were strategically thinking of ways on how we could develop more passive income that we could dump into our cash value accounts. Life was good, but the year 2008 arrived and all financial hell broke loose!!! In 2008, stocks tanked, real estate crashed, banks closed, the government had to come in and save the banking industry, mortgage and automobile industries. 2008 produced the four worst stock market drops in the history of keeping records. This was far worse for the financial markets and many compared this to the great depression of 1929. As for me and my experience, 2008 changed my financial life and gave me a new mindset in how I would proceed further in my personal life, and how I would advise my clients going forward. 2008 was terrible! My real estate investment portfolio took a gigantic hit and lost money, the mortgage brokerage company I owned had to close its doors because no mortgage company could finance any loans. I remember having mortgage loans that were closing in the coming days and receiving phone calls that no loans would be funding because mortgage companies were closing their doors. As a result of this, I had to hire an attorney and beg, or if you want to call it "negotiate", with my landlord to let me out of the remaining three years I had on the lease. I remember thinking about all the money I lost when I basically gave all the office furniture and office equipment away. I was fortunate because the landlord found a medical organization that would take over my lease, but I had to pay tremendous fees to escape the lease obligation. On top of that, home foreclosures in my community took all of the equity out of my primary home I purchased in 2005. I went from having equity in my primary home to being under water (owing more money on your home than what your home is worth) in 2008, and upon leaving my home in 2016 the value still didn't recover the highs of 2005. My retail store ownership went from three stores to one, all of my savings were depleted, I lost money in everything I owned, and the bank called in the loan on my business line of credit. All my assets were lost except one: my cash value life insurance! My cash value was the only financial vehicle I owned that didn't lose any money. As a matter of fact, it was the only financial vehicle I owned that made money, and this money allowed me to reset and recover because it carried me through the financial storm. My cash value was the only asset I owned that performed and earned interest during one of the worse financial catastrophes so, I will promote it, accumulate it, spend it, and pass it. What other financial product can provide all these advantages? My cash value life insurance allows me to experience the joys of never losing money and produces options. The more cash value I have, the more options I can take advantage of. If families everywhere obtained cash value life insurance, they could secure their financial future and build wealth now. Families would have the opportunity to build a guaranteed asset that would be in a position to provide financial protection, tax deferred growth, guaranteed appreciation, and income. Families would have available funds to take advantage of financial opportunities in real estate and the stock market and leave cash tax free for the next generation to get a head start!

There are many cash value life insurance benefits worth talking about. Cash value life insurance provide unique advantages. It is the only financial product that can provide offensive and defensive protections for your money. A good athletic team must have a good offensive and defensive strategy in order to score points and win the game. Cash value life insurance's job is to not expose you to any additional risk than what you already possess. In fact, cash value life insurance will help you reduce your exposure to all kinds of risk and provide you protection for your money throughout your lifetime! The following offensive protection advantages are obtained with using cash value life insurance: This is why I love cash value life insurance. These are the reasons why I want you to love to too:

1. **Safe** – You can't lose money!

2. **Control the flow and velocity of your money**: The flow and velocity of money is your economy; it is one of the secrets of wealth and wealth building in America. As your money moves, cash value allows it to pick up benefits you desire. You are in control.

3. **Flexibility** – Life can take many detours where you want flexibility with your money. Some of the detours will be problems, some of the detours will be opportunities. If you have flexibility you will be able to be more proactive instead of reactive. How many people do you know were blindsided by circumstances where they needed flexibility with their money and didn't have it???

4. **Accessibility** – I want you to have access to your money when you want it without any hassles or restrictions. I don't want you to have to jump through any administrative hoops to get to your money.

5. **Asset** – Your cash value is an asset. You can also use it to purchase other assets like gold, silver, real estate, stocks, or investments.

6. **Tax Free Growth** – Your money will accumulate and grow at your tax advantage.

7. **Guarantees** – No stock market risk. Cash Value earns guarantee money every year.

8. **Payment Options** – You can fund your plan to accommodate your cash flow. You can design it to pay in one payment, 7 years, 10 years, 20 years, to age 65 or for life. You have flexibility to custom design your plan.

9. **Free from Fees**– No fees will be assessed for you to participate in this program to grow your wealth.

10. **Leverage** – You can pledge your asset as collateral

11. **Less governmental control** – The Government often changes the rules. They will change the rules in the middle of the game and usually the changes are not to our benefit. The following defensive advantages are obtained with using cash value life insurance:

12. **Taxes against federal, state, capital gains, estate taxes.**

    Cash value life insurance provides the best strategies to reduce, eliminate, flatten or offset current and future taxes. Whenever you take money out of your plan you will pay no taxes.

13. **Inflation** – inflation destroys purchasing power. Cash value will allow your dollars to keep up with inflation.

14. **Liability lawsuits** – 99% of the people I see have some serious financial flaws. Cash value allows you to put a moat around your money castle.

15. **Long Term Care Services** - A feature included in life insurance policies that allows you to receive a tax-free advance on your life insurance death benefit while you are still alive. You can use this money to pay for medical care in your home. The amount of money you can receive from your policy varies, but typically the accelerated benefit payment amount is capped at 50 percent of the death benefit. Some policies, however, allow you to use the full amount of the death benefit.

16. Death – cash value life insurance will never create an economic hardship, tax, or excessive accountant or attorney fees to your family. In the event of an untimely death, cash value life insurance has the potential to create all of the money you have earned in your lifetime plus all the money you would have earned if you worked your normal career, and have that money instantly appear to your family.

It's not what cash value life insurance is, it's what cash value life insurance does. I heard it said that the perfect investment is the one that pays the most when it's needed the most. Participating dividend paying whole life insurance owned from a mutual life Insurance company is first and foremost not an investment, but a unilateral binding contract that the mutual life insurance company makes a promise to grow your cash value with guarantees. These companies will offer a return of premium to the policy owner in the form of a dividend. Dividends are not guaranteed but mutual companies have a great track record of paying dividends for 100+ years. Mutual life insurance companies are owned by their policyholders and all profits are returned to its policyholders. The more you participate, the more you earn! Participating whole life insurance has been a great cash value generator and has been a source of generational wealth accumulation since 1752. These insurance companies sell certainty. Certainty in the fact that in exchange for a premium, policyholders take the risk out of an uncertain future and replace it with future guaranteed income for 20, 30, 50, or 100+ years! Cash Value life insurance hasn't lost any money and has made money every year since its inception. The cash value is safe, liquid, guaranteed, and you pay no tax on accumulation or when a dividend is declared. The dividend will accelerate the growth of the cash value and the death benefit, and once the policy value increases it can never be lowered!

Here are the few disadvantages cash value life insurance has:

1. A disadvantage of cash value life insurance is the premiums are generally higher than term life insurance. Since cash

value life insurance policies offer lifelong coverage, they come with a higher price tag.

2. **You Have to Qualify.** Like term insurance, you are required to take a paramedical exam, which includes a blood test and urine sample. If you do not pass the life insurance underwriting criteria, your policy will be declined. And approvals can be slow with traditional fully underwritten policies, sometimes taking 6-8 weeks, or longer for approvals. To avoid this, obtain coverage when you are young and in good health.

3. If you surrender your policy too early, you can expect your cash value to be very low due to only a small percentage of your premium going into the savings account, while the rest is used to pay for upfront costs like administrative fees and the agent's commission.

4. Larger start-up costs that taper off over time. The initial fees and expenses make it difficult to get ahead in the early years of your policy. Most of the fees and expenses are front loaded into your policy. As a result, over time your policy

gets more and more efficient, paying you a higher internal rate of return the longer you have the policy.

Section 4: Conclusion

I wrote this book to bring additional awareness to communities of color to the most powerful financial product which is cash value life insurance. It is also my intention to start the conversation to create more wealth in the black community, close the wealth gap, while leaving a legacy for the next generation. It is so important to have cash value life insurance in your financial portfolio because it is the most efficient and effective way to build cash, earn interest, pay no taxes, protect your money from creditors, lawsuits, market volatility, and it allows your money to grow while simultaneously using it to build wealth.

You can't lose with the cash value life insurance I use!

My vision over the next 10 years is to help 5,000 families create enormous cash value accounts in order to take advantage of opportunities in real estate, stocks, businesses, reduce risks, and increase overall protection while building an inheritance of billions of dollars for the next generations to enjoy and repeat. Now is the time to use cash value life insurance to close the racial gap. Wealth disparity between black and white families will take 228 years to close, according to the Institute for Policy Studies. If Black Americans would use cash value life insurance as a foundational tool, this gap will close considerably. At the current pace, the problem isn't going away anytime soon. You are eligible to build cash value life insurance and leave a legacy for the next generation if you have cash, time, a good mindset, and are interested in earning compound interest for life. You are also eligible to secure your financial future and build wealth now! This is a great opportunity to build some wealth outside of the financial system, especially if you are a business owner or high earning individual looking for a smart way to save and accumulate money. Cash value life insurance is so important because it is the only financial product with a consistent track history of delivering positive results. Cash value life insurance accounts have consistently made money for the past 200+ years. It is a financial product that everyone, specifically black Americans, should have in their financial portfolio to accumulate, maximize, accelerate and grow their money. This fantastic product will enable you to build a large cash account that no one can touch but you, is a lawsuit and creditor protector, builds uninterrupted compound interest, can be designed to provide tax free income at retirement and leave a legacy for the next generation to enjoy and repeat. Contact us and we will educate you on exactly how to utilize your account and help you build cash to have opportunities for financial gains! We will look for ways to help you free up money on debt, insurance costs, taxes, and investment expenses so that you can contribute even more money to your cash value account. We will help assist you with legacy plan training so you can pass money to the next generation safely. We will stay in frequent contact with you to check in, answer questions, and show you different ways to use your account to accelerate your financial goals and help you continuously win.

My cash value is King because my cash value provides safety, guarantees, protects your money against liability and is suit protected.

You can't lose with the cash value life insurance I use - so get some!

Cash Value Affirmations

- I receive my cash value wealth in unique ways
- My cash value affords me the permission to spend my money any way I want
- My cash value can be used as a never-ending tithe to my church
- My cash value will be used to buy real estate investments
- My cash value is the moat around my financial castle
- I give thanks to my cash value because it gives me options
- My cash value floats around me continuously
- My cash value builds compound interest
- My cash value will be used to fund my next business idea

- My cash value will make me rich, wealthy and happy

- My cash value is protected against lawsuits

- My cash value helps me withdraw money out of my home that I never have to repay

- My cash value is open to the infinite supply of wealth

- My cash value will help me receive money and wealth in unique ways

- I deserve to have cash value

- I will spend my cash value while living and pass the balance to my kids at death

- My cash value is extremely prosperous, and I am deeply grateful for it

- My cash value gets better the longer I have it

- My cash value can be used as my emergency account

- My cash value can pay my kids college tuition

- My cash value can supplement my kid's college expenses

- My cash value is guaranteed to never lose money

- My cash value will earn interest every year guaranteed

- My cash value every day is getting better and better

- My cash value can pay off my credit card bills

- My cash value can allow me to replace my bank account with my favorite bank

- My cash value will help fund a scholarship in my name to my favorite university

- My cash value can fund the things I am passionate about

- My cash value gives me the permission to spend all my other assets

- My cash value can help supplement my retirement

- My cash value can offset the rising medical costs in retirement

- My cash value moves in abundant amounts in my life

- My cash value surrounds me and today I claim my share

  Life insurance is a love product. You have to love your money, or you have to love someone else. It's not what it is, it is what it does! Why not use the Internal Revenue Service tax code, guidelines, rules and regulations to accumulate as much money to spend in retirement, enjoyment, have cash to take advantage of every bad thing that will happen or give to your family, business or charity tax free? Take actionable steps now to secure your future while you can! Contact our office today to schedule a visit and learn how cash value life insurance can benefit you. We have a unique process we will use to put you in the mindset to win! We will help you with your application and help you get approved for coverage. We will design a supercharged cash value account that meets your exact needs and is tailored to your financial goals, dreams and desires.

My Cash value life insurance is King! Get Some.

For more information, visit us at

www.moorestrategy.com or contact us at (856) 642-4072